# The
# COUNTRY QUILTER'S
## Companion

# The
# *Country Quilter's*
## *Companion*

Linda Seward

Collins Publishers San Francisco
*A Division of* HarperCollins*Publishers*

First published in USA in 1994 by
Collins Publishers San Francisco
1160 Battery Street
San Francisco CA94111

First published in 1994 by Mitchell Beazley,
an imprint of Reed Consumer Books Limited, Michelin House,
81 Fulham Road, London SW3 6RB
and Auckland, Melbourne, Singapore and Toronto

Photography by James Merrell
Illustrations by Jacqueline Mair

Library of Congress Cataloging-in-Publication Data

Seward, Linda.
        The country quilter's companion / Linda Seward.
            p.    cm. -- (Country companion series)
        Includes index.
        ISBN 0-00-255366-X
        1. Quilting. 2. Patchwork. 3. Appliqué.  I. Title. II. Series.
TT835.S4577 1994
746.9'7--dc20
                                                    93-21245
                                                        CIP

Produced by Mandarin Offset
Printed and bound in China

*Page 1: An Adirondack-style twig bed flaunts a 19th-century Nine-Patch
Variation quilt, with a quilt in turkey red and white folded at its foot.
Previous page: The Autograph quilt on a bed with an appliqué Poppy quilt.*

# CONTENTS

# INTRODUCTION

*A* quilt epitomizes country style like no other single object – where something that was born of necessity has been turned into an art form. Start to decorate your surroundings with quilts and you will soon marvel at the ease with which you can give an interior a strong focus and a feeling of warmth.

Why does a quilt have such a powerful effect? Perhaps it is because by its very nature, a quilt is immensely personal. Look at an antique example and you can almost feel the presence of the woman who made it so long ago. Today, quilts are an invaluable way to ring the changes in a decorative scheme.

*Previous page: A Broken Dishes quilt on a table, with Honeycomb patchwork on the seats.*
*Right: A Mennonite Octagon quilt made in a variety of rich, dark wools.*

8

In winter, a country living room warmed by a robust log fire and furnished with richly colored quilts provides a cozy retreat from the chill outside. When summer comes, bring out lighter versions in pastel shades for a refreshing change. Quilts are versatile objects and can link color, pattern and texture in an interior, and even one good piece, thoughtfully displayed, can make a room come alive. You can display quilts by draping them over furniture, hanging them on a wall, a beam, over a banister or a quilt rack, or by placing them folded and stacked onto shelves. Also, you can frame separate antique quilt blocks to display them. Quilts invite you to wonder about their history and that of the women who made them.

*Opposite and above: Quilts may be displayed by folding and stacking them, or by hanging them over a banister. Sturdy quilts may also be used to add an extra layer of color and warmth to a chair or a sofa. Quilts seem to act as a magnet for pets, but they should be safeguarded from claws and fur. Either discourage pets from lying on quilts or else cover the quilts with protective fabric.*

# LIVING WITH QUILTS

Whether you wish to recreate an authentic country-style room from a particular period or evoke a rustic feeling in a more informal way, a quilt can serve to complete the picture of well-worn history. Carefully selected soft furnishings can provide the finishing touches to all the rooms in your home.

For instance, you can soften the hard lines of an austere room by featuring a quilt with patterned fabrics or a textured surface; give a face-lift to a sofa by tossing a sturdy quilt on top to hide sagging springs, or, if the fabric on your favorite overstuffed chair doesn't quite match the rest of the room, then try draping it

*Above: A woollen quilt, made around 1925.*
*It is backed with cotton flannel and tied with*
*yarn. The pillow is a Windmill pattern.*

*Above: Patchwork and appliqué pillows rest*
*on top of a child-size Log Cabin quilt.*
*Right: A 1930s quilt on a kitchen table.*

with a quilt in just the right colors. Quilts bought especially for snuggling should be able to stand up to some wear and tear – they should be sturdily constructed and without flaws that would be exacerbated by everyday usage.

While it is not recommended that you actually use a quilt in place of a tablecloth during a meal, covering an unused table with a quilt is an excellent way to transform the heart of your home into a warm, cozy and inviting place.

*Right: Fresh flowers and painted lattice-work harmonize with an 1860s English quilt made in pastel shades. The quilt gives the guest bedroom the feeling of a gentle summer's day.*

*The square patches of this quilt are made from men's cotton shirting and sprigged print fabrics. This is a typical example of the everyday quilts that were made in the mid-19th century.*

The stout-hearted reliability of a well-made practical quilt adds character to a decorating scheme. However, you should save the more fragile antique quilts for display only, in areas that are not subject to so much use.

If you have an unsightly metal radiator that is no longer in use but is too expensive to remove, try arranging a quilt over it to make it into a feature. In the same way you can rejuvenate an old chest by covering it with a quilt.

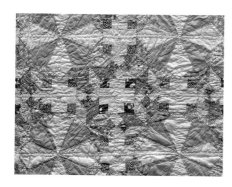

*Above: Pure cotton, both plain or printed, is an ideal material for constructing quilts. Right: A Turkey Tracks quilt on the split rail fence shows years of wear in the frayed patches, yet it retains its dignity. Dating from around 1880, it was made in Knox County, Tennessee, of linsey, a hand-woven cloth of wool and cotton, so named because originally it had linen as the warp thread.*

There are many ways to display a quilt spontaneously. A child-size quilt would be a naive and charming alternative to a table runner. A collection of framed patchwork blocks would be a simple yet bright solution to a dark hallway.

If you possess a damaged quilt you can fold it at the foot of a bed to conceal any tattered parts. Several quilts folded and stacked on shelves give the impression of a generous collection and add color and interest to a room.

Pillows and cushions are probably the most popular country-style accessories. Patchwork, appliqué or quilted, tossed on a sofa, heaped in a mountain on a bed or artfully arranged on a chair, they will add the perfect finishing touch to every room in the house.

Hanging a quilt on a wall is the most obvious way to display a textile other than as a bed covering. Ensure that the quilt isn't too old and that it is well-stitched and robust so that the pressure of hanging doesn't cause sagging or deterioration. When you buy a quilt to hang on a wall, you need to think about it in

*Above left: A 19th-century red and white Pineapple quilt draped over an upholstered chair gives an extra layer of comfort. The "pineapple" shapes are created by sewing strips of fabrics around a center triangle.*
*Left: Soft pastel lavender and crisp white fabrics have been used to create this charming Double Irish Chain quilt made in New Jersey around 1930. Floral wreaths are quilted in the white blocks in between the "chains", while the chain itself is outline-quilted.*

the same way that you would consider a painting you are thinking of buying. Study the border carefully, as it will serve to frame the quilt on the wall. Suspending a quilt against a wall that delicately echoes one of the quilt's own colors will bring out the best in both. Never hang a quilt above a mantel unless the fireplace is not in use.

If you are holding an outdoor party, it would be charming to drape quilts over railings on a veranda or a porch to make your guests feel welcome. It is best to position the quilts in the shade or in dappled sunlight.

*Above: The rough wooden walls of a rustic cabin contrast well with the crisp white and navy blue fabrics in this 1890s patchwork quilt. The colors are an appropriate choice since the pattern is called Ocean Waves; the quilt was made in West Virginia.*
*Left: Stars are popular quilt motifs. Here a Rolling Star quilt hangs on a wall. A hanging quilt should be brought down and allowed to "rest" for the same length of time that the quilt was left hanging.*

# PATCHWORK

*P*atchwork is an age-old method of quilt-making where individual pieces of cloth, in all manner of shapes, colors, sizes and textures, are sewn together to create a whole piece. Consider that many women who laboriously stitched quilts in the past were uneducated in mathematics and geometry; how did they conceive such myriad designs? Generations of quilters have handed down literally hundreds of patchwork configurations and so left a rich legacy of designs, from perfect geometric stars to haphazard Crazy patterns.

*Previous page: An English Honeycomb quilt made*
*from dress fabrics, around 1840.*
*Left: A Honeycomb patchwork wall hanging,*
*which is probably the middle of an unfinished quilt.*

21

# PIECED BLOCK

*A* block is a single design unit which is usually square or rectangular in shape. Individual blocks of patchwork or appliqué are pieced either by sewing them together or else by joining the edges with strips of sashing. A repeat pattern composed of rows of pieced blocks sewn together creates a quilt top.

The block method evolved partly as a space-saving device which precluded the need for continually adding to a cumbersome and ever-expanding quilt. Geometric images were assembled into blocks and then repeated.

With all the equipment and beautiful fabrics that are available today, as well as

*Below left: A glowing mid 19th-century quilt from New York State; the maker of this rare piece may have taken her inspiration from the delightfully named Lady Fingers and Sunflowers design or Whig's Defeat.*
*Right: Partly folding a quilt for display on a chair or a table can artfully conceal areas of the piece which may be damaged. The Half Moon Rising design was made in South Carolina at the turn of the century. The woollen Welsh quilt folded on the ottoman is a Variable Star design with Prince of Wales feather quilting; it dates from 1880.*

the leisure time to spend on a project, you'd think it would be easy to duplicate, if not surpass, the sewing skills that are displayed on old quilts. But if you start to make a traditional patchwork quilt, your respect for the original designer will grow with every seam that you sew. Ponder the thought that the time for quilt-making was eked out from the hundreds of other domestic tasks that women were expected to accomplish every day; however bone-weary they may have been, they still had enough energy left at the end of the day to add a few more stitches to their quilts.

An antique patchwork quilt made by an expert needlewoman will be well-pieced and show matching seams and smoothly fitting pieces. Quilts with a folk-art quality will often be irregularly pieced which only adds to their charm. As a general rule, the more intricate the piecing, the more valuable the quilt. Bargain quilts may still be found at flea markets, garage sales and auctions, but take great care in examining the quilt to

make sure that it is in good condition. More expensive but probably higher in quality are the quilts for sale in quilt shops, antique shops and through quilt dealers. It is always fascinating to find out about the history of any quilt that you buy – who made it, where was it made, and was it made for a special reason such as a birth, a wedding or a farewell? Knowing a quilt's history will not only add to its value, but will also add to your pleasure in owning this small piece of the past. For instance, strong social ties were expressed through needlework. Autograph quilts came into existence as a way for a society to raise money for a specific cause. Signees contributed anywhere from five cents to five dollars to autograph a quilt and once it was finished it was auctioned for additional funds, or perhaps given to a prominent local person.

blocks were sewn together before being presented as a gift to a bride or an outstanding member of the community. The freedom quilt was a variation on the same theme and was made for a young man by his female relatives and acquaintances when he reached his coming of age birthday. A number of benevolent societies made quilts to give to the poor, send to missionaries or to auction for some charitable purpose.

*Below left: Square in Square blocks on an 1880s quilt made in Tennessee. The patchwork design is also called Twelve Diamonds.*

*Above left: A 1920s Bear's Paw quilt. Below: In front, a Rocky Road to Kansas quilt and, behind, a Broken Dishes quilt.*

Friends and neighbors often stitched and pieced blocks into a variety of friendship quilts. Each patchwork or appliqué block was stitched by a different person and sometimes inscribed with a relevant saying, or perhaps the name of the local town and the date of a departure. The blocks were then assembled into a farewell quilt and presented to a woman or a family who was leaving the community. Album quilts fulfilled a similar purpose and individually worked

*Below: A Shoo Fly quilt draped on the rocking chair and, behind,*
*a Crown of Thorns quilt hung over the deck railing.*

*Below: A T-block quilt hangs from a gallery. A Tulip quilt lies on the table and two chairs are upholstered in Whig's Defeat design woven fabric.*

# LOG CABIN

*T*he Log Cabin design derived its name from the American pioneer tradition of building rural dwellings from rough-hewn logs. As women began moving west across North America in the mid-19th century, their quilts served many functions along the way. For instance, they were used to pack precious dishes and other breakable objects, they were folded to act as pillows on the hard wooden seats of covered wagons during the journey, they protected the sides of the wagons during Indian attacks and they served as the family's bedding at night. More somberly, quilts were also used to bury those who perished during the arduous journey west. Instead of leaving the corpse in an unmourned grave, the pioneers wrapped it in one of their best quilts for burial.

*Right: A painted wooden Swedish blanket chest houses a pair of colorful turn-of-the-century Log Cabin quilts.*
*Below: This detail of a Log Cabin pattern shows the unusual technique of covering the seams with embroidery.*

*Above: The traditional central red squares of the Log Cabin quilt are clearly visible on this example, displayed on an authentic rope bed.*

# STARS

*O*ne of the earliest and most popular single images in the quilting world is the star. Hundreds of different star designs have been developed, changed, copied and improved upon over the years on both sides of the Atlantic. The star itself can have five, six, eight points or more, and some "star" designs do not actually resemble stars at all!

Probably the most popular and also the simplest to construct is called Ohio Star. This design is composed of a single large square surrounded by eight triangular points. The Variable Star is an adaptation of this design, although the central square is turned on point in order to give an added dimension.

Quilt patterns have immortalized famous people as well as those who would not normally have left their mark on society. However, no commemorative pattern has been so popular as that named after the two brothers who founded New Orleans in 1718. Jean Baptiste and Pierre Le Moyne were honored by the Le Moyne Star, subsequently changed to Lemoyne Star and then corrupted in New England to

*Left: The blue and white Lone Star quilt on the table in this dining room dates from around 1930 and was made in Missouri; the diamond patchwork binding adds an unusual touch. Lone Star quilts can be found in good condition because many were made as "best" quilts. As such, they were only brought out and put on display for special occasions.*
*Right: In a hallway, an unused radiator is cloaked with a magnificent silk Star of Bethlehem quilt and acts as a shelf for the owner's antique English quilts.*

Lemon Star. This is one of the oldest star designs and its diamond-pieced construction is the foundation of countless variations on the star theme.

As America was colonized, the endurance of hardship was a fact of life that turned many people toward religion. And what better way was there to celebrate their faith than through the creation of a quilt based on a religious symbol? The Bible inspired hundreds of quilt designs, and one of the best-loved was the Star of Bethlehem, also known as the Lone Star, which was widely adopted in homes both as prize pieces and as more everyday bed coverings. It is one of the most dramatic quilt patterns and shows a huge star ablaze with color and set against a contrasting background, which often serves to make the star glow. It is frequently surrounded by intricate appliqué or quilting.

*Below left: An 1850s Seven Stars quilt made by a pioneer. Right: Dramatic red sashing separates the large Evening Star blocks on this 1950s North Carolina quilt which is draped over a hickory chair.*

*Below: Gossamer drapes and rough wooden walls are the perfect backdrop for this Spinning Stars scrap quilt, made in Texas around 1840. The whole design appears to vibrate with movement.*

*Above: This Ohio Star quilt which hangs over a porch rail is a simple composition of a large square surrounded by eight triangular points.*

*Above: A magnificent Lone Star quilt competes successfully with the surrounding Tennessee woods; it was made in Memphis around 1880.*

# SCHOOLHOUSE

$Q$uilt designs were inspired by all sorts of daily experiences including religion, domestic life, nature, work, agriculture, politics and the community. As a result, everyday objects and occurrences were incorporated into designs which were often given lyrical names, for instance, Whig's Defeat, Love Apple, Cherry Basket, Monkey Wrench, Wild Goose Chase and Drunkard's Path. Likewise, social events brought about designs such as Barn Raising and Hands All Around. By the same token, for pioneers living in scattered frontier settlements across North America, significant buildings such as churches, log cabins and schoolhouses symbolized the establishment of a stable community and were often taken as decorative themes by quiltmakers of the past. Individual blocks sewn with a variety of geometric patches – depicting the walls, windows, roof,

*Below left: A Schoolhouse pillow blends with patriotic pillows on a breezy country-style porch in New York State.*

*Right: The Schoolhouse design evokes a country mood like no other pattern. This quilt was hand-pieced and tufted in Vermont, around 1880.*

chimney and front door of a schoolhouse – were pieced together in order to form a simple repeat pattern.

Although quilts were originally made as utilitarian bedcoverings, they evolved into much more than that. A woman's most prized attribute was her skill with a needle, and this everyday activity turned bedcovers into works of art that were admired by family and friends, and later achieved recognition at country fairs and contests.

Some examples were so prized that fine pieces were used for dowries and trousseaus, and were even given as payment in years when the crops failed.

Quilt-making in America was a highly social activity where neighbors gathered together in groups known as quilting bees. Some quilting bees lasted several days – the hostess would usually supply thread and scissors and guests would sit around a giant quilting frame, stitching and exchanging gossip.

# CRAZY QUILTS

Quilts and quilted accessories can strike a country mood in almost any setting. The appropriately named Crazy quilt is a kaleidoscopic patchwork design which is composed of a random arrangement of unevenly shaped pieces of fabric. It is believed to be one of the earliest forms of piecing cloth together. Original Crazy quilts were little more than utilitarian patchwork blankets made from clothing and worn scraps, which were all sewn onto a foundation.

As well as irregular patches and eye-catching color schemes, Crazy quilts show a variety of contrasting textures. Pieces of velvet, silk, wool, rich brocades and cotton blend happily side by side and are often embellished with brightly colored embroidery, which also serves to hide unsightly edges.

*Left: A Victorian Crazy quilt and teddy bear, made in Pennsylvania, around 1880.*
*Right: A utilitarian Crazy Quilt made around 1910. The blocks pieced together show a muted palette of cotton and woollen fabrics.*
*Below: Decorative stitching hides the raw edges of a colorful Crazy patchwork quilt.*

At the turn of the century, Crazy quilts became a fashionable alternative to the much more strictly geometric designs that had dominated before.

But because these quilts were made more to establish a woman's credentials as a fine needleworker than to keep members of her family warm at night, they were displayed throughout the home for all to admire. This is the first instance where "quilts" were openly used as decorative objects instead of being hidden from view in the bedroom or in a hope chest. The opulent fabrics and intricate embroidery perfectly complemented the ornamental theme of the late 19th century, when Crazy quilts were particularly popular.

# Appliqué

Appliqué is the method of applying and securing one piece of fabric on top of another. This decorative technique has been adopted for many purposes, from adorning heraldic banners to embellishing magnificent Baltimore Album quilts. In the mid-19th century women in the Baltimore area produced a host of appliqué designs depicting birds, wreaths, garlands of flowers, baskets of fruits and even public buildings and important monuments. Many of these patterns are still regarded as the quintessential appliqué designs.

*Previous page: An 1890s Princess Feather quilt from North Carolina makes an elegant wall-hanging.*
*Right: The North Carolina Lily quilt boasts appliqué and patchwork. It was probably made in Illinois around 1880.*

# FLORAL

*Right: Many quilts feature motifs inspired by nature. Below: A Tulip appliqué made in the late 1800s from Davidson County, and the Tree of Life made around 1920.*

*Right: A Tree of Life quilt and a Primitive Flower quilt hang from a beam. On the chair below is a Love Apple quilt made in Iowa. In front is a patchwork Monkey Wrench quilt.*

Women living on the east coast of America began to enjoy more leisure time to devote to their needlework in the latter half of the 19th century. Patchwork quilts, other than masterpieces, were looked upon as utilitarian items and so women turned their skills and attention to making intricate appliqué designs. Appliqué allowed for more freedom in design than patchwork. The applied shapes were drawn freehand and so they assumed all sorts of

*Above: The rose appeared in all sorts of guises in quilt design. The lightweight 19th-century Rose Wreath quilt on the simple wooden bed was used as a summer counter-pane and was backed but not quilted. Right: A Double Tulip quilt on the canopy bed was probably a "best" quilt. The bedside table is draped with a Posies Round the Square quilt to match the bedcover.*

representational forms. Also, there was no need to fit the pieces together in a neat jigsaw-fashion. Hundreds of patterns celebrated the beauty of nature.

Floral appliqué was especially popular during the 1850s and 1860s, and classical designs incorporating wreaths and urns were also fashionable. Flowers as well as fruits and berries were typically worked in shades of red, green and white. Bridal quilts depicted all kinds of rose motifs as well as the popular Rose of Sharon variations. And foliage also provided inspiration, giving rise to designs such as Hickory Leaf, Mountain Laurel and Pride of the Forest.

*Above: A collection of American appliqué quilts, dating from around 1850. In the top right-hand corner is a cot quilt; in the bottom right-hand corner the use of small-print fabrics produces a pretty flower basket design.*
*Left: Some 1930s appliqué quilts. The top left example has a central tree of life motif; the quilt below shows individual pictorial motifs, while the other two examples resemble pieced quilts with their even patterns.*

# QUILTING

$N$o matter how elaborately pieced or appliquéd a quilt may be, it only comes to life when the quilting stitches are added. The small, regular stitches not only delineate a quilt's pattern but also hold the layers firmly together. Our forebears succeeded in turning quilting into a fine art. On some of the antique quilts illustrated in this book the tiny, even quilting stitches are as many as 18 to the inch. However, the padding in old quilts is thinner than is used today and because women began to sew at an early age they had plenty of practice!

*Previous page: A pair of wedding quilts known as* courtepointes *on rustic painted chairs from Provence; they were made around 1850.*
*Right: The Whig's Defeat pattern commemorates the Whig Party, which lasted from about 1832 to 1852 and stood for the common man.*

# NORTH COUNTRY

*T*hroughout the second half of the 19th century and into the 20th century quilts were in conventional use in most homes in the north of England. The cold climate and economic times meant that making a bed quilt was a necessary part of life. The quilts that took pride of place were known as "wholecloth" quilts – they were made from plain lengths of fabric which showed off the delicacy of the quilting stitches to perfection. Patchwork was out of favor and so rarely

used for the front of a quilt, just the back, and only then out of absolute necessity. Making a wholecloth quilt was an excellent way for a woman to show off her needlework prowess and the smallest details were scrutinized – each curve was perfect, every stitch was tiny and even. White cloth was considered the ideal background for quilting, as there was nothing to detract from the flawlessness of the stitches.

Although many wholecloth, heavily quilted pieces are known collectively as "Durham quilts", they were in fact not only produced in this small county in the northeast of England, but were made throughout the surrounding area, as well as in Scotland and Wales. It was at this time that expert quilters and pattern-makers came into their own.

Professional quilt stampers would charge a fee to stamp the full design of a wholecloth quilt on the plain fabric so that the quilter could then follow the markings and begin stitching. The most talented stampers, such as George Gardiner and Elizabeth Sanderson, became household names and their quilts have an easily recognizable and distinctive style.

*Left: The sturdy Bordered Star quilt from Durham is in the style of Elizabeth Sanderson, who may have marked it. The cheerful red and white scheme is echoed in the Strippy Sawtooth quilt on the daybed below.*

*Left: On the left is a Durham Basket quilt, dating from around 1900; it was quilted by Elizabeth Sanderson. The unusual Circles and Crescents quilt on the right was made around 1850, also in Durham.*

Traditionally, the fabrics that were most favored for North Country quilts were cotton or sateen, generally in white or cream, or perhaps dyed a darker shade with a lighter shade on the reverse side. A typical design would feature a central medallion filled with flowers, leaves and curved running feathers, a twisted cable pattern or a series of hammock designs.

In America, the equivalent was the White Work quilt where the all-white surface called for refined stitching executed by the most experienced fingers. The single medallion remained at the

*Right: Durham or "wholecloth" quilts are characterized by a white or a cream background, which gives prominence to the quality of the stitching. Close quilting is essential in order to prevent the filling inside from shifting.*

*Right: This cream sateen quilt has a bordered design reminiscent of the style of the pattern-stamper George Gardiner. The central medallion is filled with flowers and feathers. The quilt at the foot of the bed is called Devil's Claws.*

perhaps a lover's knot, set against a background with a diamond infill pattern. The corners were often embellished with fans, roses, bells or a design known as cocks comb. The whole piece might be bordered with magnificent heart of the design and the rest was elegantly quilted and often corded and stuffed. Such quilts were probably only worked on during daylight hours, when there was optimum light, and often took years to complete.

# CORDING & TRAPUNTO

*T*rapunto, which is also known as stuffed quilting, is one of the most admired forms of quilting. It is a painstaking technique which is worked by sewing two layers of plain fabric together and creating a design which is then stuffed from the wrong side so that the design stands out in high relief. The three-dimensional effect of Trapunto quilts relies on using loose-weave fabric so that the threads can be separated without tearing them; the filling is then inserted through the opening and the threads pushed back into their original position. This form of raised quilting is often enhanced by close filling stitches which serve to flatten the background, so causing the stuffed areas to stand out. Corded quilting produces a similar sculptural effect and derives its name because a length of cord is threaded in-between parallel lines of running stitches. Both techniques date back to medieval times and were a popular means of decorating the clothing and furnishings of the wealthy. By the 18th century stuffed quilting was introduced to America, and not long afterward well-to-do ladies living in the northeast and southern parts of the country were creating extremely fine examples of all-white Trapunto quilts.

*Left: This Trapunto quilt with a cream back-ground is livened up with a sprinkling of small black dots. The folded quilt blends perfectly with the surrounding textures of natural stone, cream plasterwork, rugs and rushwork.*
*Right: The fabrics in the glowing quilts shown here are from Provence in southern France, which is also where the quilts were made in about 1880. The stunning example draped over the bench has been corded and stuffed.*

# CARE

$A$ quilt will receive the least amount of stress when it is kept flat, so one of the best ways to store or display a prized quilt is to place it on a bed. You can also exhibit a quilt by folding it. You should then refold it two or three times a year to take the strain away from the folds: if the folds are left for too long then the fibers will weaken. In the same way, quilts that are hung up on a wall must be allowed to rest for a length of time equal to that which they spent hanging, so as to ease the strain on the threads. Shake out and air a quilt regularly.

*Previous page: Typical examples of late 19th-century American patchwork and appliqué quilts are carefully stored in a pie safe.*
*Right: These early American quilts are folded and stacked in a linen press; the wing chair is upholstered in a Whig's Defeat fabric.*

*Above: Resting on wooden chairs are a Nosegay quilt*
*Variation quilt. Quilts are portable soft furnishings an o*
*in an open-air setting. However, do not expose quilts z*
*as this will cause fading; they should only be used z*

*Above: Resting on wooden chairs are a Nosegay quilt and a Sawtooth Variation quilt. Quilts are portable soft furnishings and may be utilized in an open-air setting. However, do not expose quilts to direct sunlight as this will cause fading; they should only be used in the shade.*

*Right: This 1930s doll quilt laid on the schoolmaster's desk was made from wool scraps and yarn. Below left: A Toad in a Puddle quilt made in the 1840s, in New York State.*

*Below right: A Double Nine-Patch quilt graces the Adirondack-style twig bed and a Variable Star quilt is folded at its foot. Patchwork pillows enhance the effect.*

Avoid exposing a quilt to strong sunlight as the fabrics will fade. Do not allow water or damp to come into contact with a quilt. Protect quilts from damage caused by insects, rodents and pets. Keep a quilt dust-free by low-suction vacuuming. Store quilts wrapped in a cotton pillowcase in a dry place.

# INDEX